Jon

A

love

Annette & Neil
xx

Wit of the Nation

Richard Benson

summersdale

WIT OF THE NATION

Copyright © Summersdale Publishers Ltd 2007

No part of this book may be reproduced by any means, nor transmitted, nor translated into a machine language, without the written permission of the publishers.

Condition of Sale
This book is sold subject to the condition that it shall not, by way of trade or otherwise, be lent, re-sold, hired out or otherwise circulated in any form of binding or cover other than that in which it is published and without a similar condition including this condition being imposed on the subsequent publisher.

Summersdale Publishers Ltd
46 West Street
Chichester
West Sussex
PO19 1RP
UK

www.summersdale.com

Printed and bound in Finland by WS Bookwell.

Disclaimer
Every effort has been made to attribute the quotations in this collection to the correct source. Should there be any omissions or errors in this respect we apologise and shall be pleased to make the appropriate acknowledgements in any future editions.

ISBN: 1-84024-620-0
ISBN 13: 978-1-84024-620-9

Wit of
the Nation

Richard Benson

Contents

Editor's Note

When it comes to belly-aching witticisms, no one does it quite like the Brits.

This wonderful nation has been witness to centuries of dry politicians, cut-throat comedians, hilarious writers and a whole host of other fabulously funny people just waiting to be quoted by the rest of us.

There comes a time when we're all looking for that classic one-liner to brighten up a dull wedding speech, impart knowledge to our children or simply make us sound far funnier than we actually are. If that time is now, you're holding the right book.

To save you trawling through a lifetime of literature, we've compiled the cream of the cackle-worthy crop for you to feast on. Nestled in the pages of this quotable collection are wry remarks, poignant ponderings and ticklesome treats to suit all manner of occasions.

Neatly organised into subject sections ranging from families, friends and foreigners to manners, money and media, the hardest thing left for you to do is pick your favourites.

So sit back, relax and prepare to free your stiff upper lip – a good old British smirk is just a page away.

ANIMAL INSTINCTS

A horse is dangerous
at both ends and
uncomfortable
in the middle.

Ian Fleming

A dog is not intelligent.
Never trust an animal that's
surprised by its own farts.

Frank Skinner

I have a memory like an elephant. In
fact, elephants often consult me.

Noël Coward

Dogs look up to us. Cats look
down on us. Pigs treat us as equals.

Winston Churchill

I am an evil giraffe, and I shall eat more leaves from this tree than perhaps I should, so that other giraffes may die.

Eddie Izzard

If a dog jumps in your lap, it is because he is fond of you; but if a cat does the same thing, it is because your lap is warmer.

Alfred North Whitehead

If an army of monkeys were
strumming on typewriters,
they might write all the books
in the British Museum.

Arthur Eddington

Cats have nine lives. Which makes
them ideal for experimentation.

Jimmy Carr

Man is an animal that makes
bargains: no other animal
does this – no dog exchanges
bones with another.

Adam Smith

Animals are such agreeable friends – they ask no questions, they pass no criticisms.

George Eliot

—•—

You think dogs will not be in heaven? I tell you, they will be there long before any of us.

Robert Louis Stevenson

—•—

When my cats aren't happy, I'm not happy. Not because I care about their mood but because I know they're just sitting there thinking up ways to get even.

Percy Bysshe Shelley

If somebody thinks they're a
hedgehog, presumably you just
give 'em a mirror and a few pictures
of hedgehogs and tell them to
sort it out for themselves.

Douglas Adams

Dogs come when they're
called; cats take a message
and get back to you later.

Eloisa James

Deer hunting would be fine sport,
if only the deer had guns.

William S. Gilbert

The great pleasure of a dog is that you may make a fool of yourself with him and not only will he not scold you, but he will make a fool of himself too.

Samuel Butler

———•———

No human being, however great, or powerful, was ever so free as a fish.

John Ruskin

———•———

The cat could very well be man's best friend but would never stoop to admitting it.

Doug Larson

If a donkey bray at you,
don't bray at him.

George Herbert

When the eagles are silent,
the parrots begin to jabber.

Winston Churchill

If you eliminate smoking
and gambling, you
will be amazed to
find that almost all an
Englishman's pleasures
can be, and mostly are,
shared by his dog.

George Bernard Shaw

ARTISTIC LICENCE

It is not hard to
understand modern
art. If it hangs on a wall
it's a painting, and if
you can walk around
it it's a sculpture.

Tom Stoppard

The length of a film should be
directly related to the endurance
of the human bladder.

Alfred Hitchcock

Art, like morality, consists of
drawing the line somewhere.

G. K. Chesterton

Acting is merely the art of keeping a
large group of people from coughing.

Ralph Richardson

Rules and models destroy
genius and art.

William Hazlitt

Acting is not very hard. The
most important things are to
be able to laugh and cry.

Glenda Jackson

Fine art is that in which the
hand, the head, and the heart
of man go together.

John Ruskin

Spielberg isn't a film-maker,
he's a confectioner.

Alex Cox

The buttocks are the most
aesthetically pleasing part of
the body because they are non-
functional. Although they conceal
an essential orifice, these pointless
globes are as near as the human
form can ever come to abstract art.

Kenneth Tynan

Anything simple
always interests me.

David Hockney

Writing about music is like dancing about architecture – it's a really stupid thing to want to do.

Elvis Costello

I know not, sir, whether Bacon wrote the works of Shakespeare, but if he did not it seems to me that he missed the opportunity of his life.

J. M. Barrie

History has remembered the kings and warriors because they destroyed; art has remembered the people because they created.

William Morris

Lying in bed would be an altogether
perfect and supreme experience
if only one had a coloured pencil
long enough to draw on the ceiling.

G. K. Chesterton

You just pick up a chord, go
twang, and you've got music.

Sid Vicious

Without tradition, art is a flock
of sheep without a shepherd.
Without innovation, it is a corpse.

Winston Churchill

A jazz musician is a juggler who uses
harmonies instead of oranges.

Benny Green

The moral of film-making in
Britain is that you will be
screwed by the weather.

Hugh Grant

When love and skill work together,
expect a masterpiece.

John Ruskin

Music is the wine that fills
the cup of silence.

Robert Fripp

It is a mistake for a sculptor or
a painter to speak or write very
often about his job. It releases
tension needed for his work.

Henry Moore

I understand the inventor of the
bagpipes was inspired when he
saw a man carrying an indignant,
asthmatic pig under his arm.
Unfortunately, the man-made
sound never equalled the purity of
the sound achieved by the pig.

Alfred Hitchcock

Comedy is simply a funny
way of being serious.

Peter Ustinov

BEING BEAUTIFUL

The problem with beauty is that it's like being born rich and getting poorer.

Joan Collins

Remember that the most
beautiful things in the world
are the most useless; peacocks
and lilies, for example.

John Ruskin

Beauty is all very well at first sight;
but whoever looks at it when it has
been in the house three days?

George Bernard Shaw

Beauty is an ecstasy; it is as
simple as hunger. There is really
nothing to be said about it. It is
like the perfume of a rose: you
can smell it and that is all.

W. Somerset Maugham

A witty woman is a treasure;
a witty beauty is a power.

George Meredith

To look almost pretty is an
acquisition of higher delight
to a girl who has been looking
plain for the first 15 years of
her life than a beauty from her
cradle can ever receive.

Jane Austen

How goodness
heightens beauty!

Hannah More

Beauty is an outward gift which is seldom despised, except by those to whom it has been refused.

Edward Gibbon

You can take no credit for beauty at 16. But if you are beautiful at 60, it will be your soul's own doing.

Marie Stopes

The best part of beauty is that which no picture can express.

Francis Bacon

It is hard, if not impossible, to snub
a beautiful woman – they remain
beautiful and the snub recoils.

Winston Churchill

The absence of flaw in
beauty is itself a flaw.

Henry Havelock Ellis

A poor beauty finds more
lovers than husbands.

George Herbert

The saying that beauty is but
skin-deep is but a skin-deep saying.

John Ruskin

Love built on beauty,
soon as beauty, dies.

John Donne

The human soul needs actual
beauty more than bread.

D. H. Lawrence

Beauty is Nature's coin,
must not be hoarded,
But must be current.

John Milton

—◆—

Against the beautiful and the
clever and the successful, one
can wage a pitiless war, but not
against the unattractive: then the
millstone weighs on the breast.

Graham Greene

—◆—

It is well known that Beauty does
not look with a good grace on
the timid advances of Humour.

W. Somerset Maugham

A bachelor never quite gets
over the idea that he is a thing
of beauty and a boy forever.

Helen Rowland

Plainness has its peculiar
temptations quite as much as beauty.

George Eliot

Nonsense and beauty have
close connections.

E. M. Forster

———•———

Familiarity is a magician that is cruel
to beauty but kind to ugliness.

Ouida

———•———

It is only shallow people who do
not judge by appearances.

Oscar Wilde

BEST OF BRITISH

My children are not royal; they just happen to have the Queen for their aunt.

Princess Margaret

It took me 20 years of studied self-restraint, aided by the natural decay of my faculties, to make myself dull enough to be accepted as a serious person by the British public.

George Bernard Shaw

The English contribution to world cuisine – the chip.

John Cleese

A tree might be a show in Scotland as a horse in Venice.

Samuel Johnson

An Irishman fights before he reasons, a Scotchman reasons before he fights, an Englishman is not particular as to the order of precedence, but will do either to accommodate his customers.

Charles Caleb Colton

The land of embarrassment and breakfast.

Julian Barnes on Britain

American-style iced tea is the
perfect drink for a hot, sunny
day. It's never really caught on
in the UK, probably because
the last time we had a hot,
sunny day was back in 1957.

Tom Holt

❧

As a rule they will refuse even to
sample a foreign dish, they regard
such things as garlic and olive oil
with disgust, life is unliveable to them
unless they have tea and puddings.

George Orwell

The monarchy is so extraordinarily useful. When Britain wins a battle she shouts, 'God save the Queen'; when she loses she votes down the prime minister.

Winston Churchill

The whole strength of England lies in the fact that the enormous majority of the English people are snobs.

George Bernard Shaw

When I told the people of
Northern Ireland that I was an
atheist, a woman in the audience
stood up and said, 'Yes, but
is it the god of the Catholics
or the god of the Protestants
in whom you don't believe?'

Quentin Crisp

Oats. A grain, which in England
is generally given to horses, but in
Scotland supports the people.

Samuel Johnson

The Irish are hearty, the Scotch plausible, the French polite, the Germans good-natured, the Italians courtly, the Spaniards reserved and decorous – the English alone seem to exist in taking and giving offence.

William Hazlitt

I've sometimes thought... that the difference between us and the English is that the Scotch are hard in all other respects but soft with women, and the English are hard with women but soft in all other respects.

J. M. Barrie

If the English language made
any sense, lackadaisical would
have something to do with
a shortage of flowers.

Doug Larson

One has often wondered whether
upon the whole earth there is
anything so unintelligent, so
unapt to perceive how the world is
really going, as an ordinary young
Englishman of our upper class.

Matthew Arnold

What Englishman will give his mind to politics as long as he can afford to keep a motor car?

George Bernard Shaw

I think the British have the distinction above all other nations of being able to put new wine into old bottles without bursting them.

Clement Attlee

There's nothing the British like better than a bloke who comes from nowhere, makes it, and then gets clobbered.

Melvyn Bragg

It is illegal in England to
state in print that a wife can
and should derive sexual
pleasure from intercourse.

Bertrand Russell

The British do not expect
happiness. I had the impression,
all the time that I lived there,
that they do not want to be
happy; they want to be right.

Quentin Crisp

Scotland: a land of meanness,
sophistry and lust.

Lord Byron

Only in Britain could it be thought a defect to be 'too clever by half'. The probability is that too many people are too stupid by three-quarters.

John Major

———

What two ideas are more inseparable than beer and Britannia?

Sydney Smith

———

The maxim of the British people is 'Business as usual.'

Winston Churchill

BETWEEN THE SHEETS

The Englishman can
get along with sex
quite perfectly so long
as he can pretend
that it isn't sex but
something else.

James Agate

For flavour, instant sex will never supersede the stuff you have to peel and cook.

Quentin Crisp

◆

There is hardly anyone whose sexual life, if it were broadcast, would not fill the world at large with surprise and horror.

W. Somerset Maugham

◆

You have to see the sex act comically, as a child.

W. H. Auden

I've only slept with men I've been married to. How many women can make that claim?

Elizabeth Taylor

Sex – the great inequality, the great miscalculator, the great irritator.

Enid Bagnold

If someone had told me years ago that sharing a sense of humour was so vital to partnerships, I could have avoided a lot of sex.

Kate Beckinsale

Quite frankly, if you bed
people of below-stairs class,
they go to the papers.

Jane Clark

Make love to every woman you
meet; if you get five per cent of
your outlay it's a good investment.

Arnold Bennett

Sex is the last refuge of the miserable.

Quentin Crisp

The human race has been set up. Someone, somewhere, is playing a practical joke on us. Apparently, women need to feel loved to have sex. Men need to have sex to feel loved. How do we ever get started?

Billy Connolly

Older women are best, because they always think they may be doing it for the last time.

Ian Fleming

I'm a sex machine to both genders. It's all very exhausting. I need a lot of sleep.

Rupert Everett

Continental people have sex lives;
the English have hot-water bottles.

Georges Mikes

Q

The war between the sexes is
the only one in which both sides
regularly sleep with the enemy.

Quentin Crisp

Q

I know it does make people
happy, but to me it is just
like having a cup of tea.

Cynthia Paine

All this fuss about sleeping together. For physical pleasure I'd sooner go to my dentist any day.

Evelyn Waugh

You know, of course, that the Tasmanians, who never committed adultery, are now extinct.

W. Somerset Maugham

Pornography is the attempt to
insult sex, to do dirt on it.

D. H. Lawrence

Sex is a short cut to everything.

Anne Cumming

BOOKS AND BEYOND

Writing is easy. You only need to stare at a piece of blank paper until your forehead bleeds.

Douglas Adams

Some books are to be tasted,
others to be swallowed, and some
few to be chewed and digested.

Francis Bacon

Literature is mostly about having
sex and not much about having
children; life is the other way round.

David Lodge

I've always believed in writing without
a collaborator, because where
two people are writing the same
book, each believes he gets all the
worries and only half the royalties.

Agatha Christie

I hate vulgar realism in literature.
The man who could call a spade a
spade should be compelled to use
one. It is the only thing he is fit for.

Oscar Wilde

—◆—

Literature is the art of writing
something that will be read twice;
journalism will be grasped at once.

Cyril Connolly

A pen is to me as a
beak is to a hen.

J. R. R. Tolkien

No human being ever spoke of scenery for above two minutes at a time, which makes me suspect that we hear too much of it in literature.

Robert Louis Stevenson

How little our libraries cost us as compared with our liquor cellars.

John Lubbock

A historical romance is the only kind of book where chastity really counts.

Barbara Cartland

The closest you will ever
come in this life to an orderly
universe is a good library.

Ashleigh Brilliant

The closest you will ever
come in this life to an orderly

Better to write for yourself and
have no public, than to write for
the public and have no self.

Cyril Connolly

I take the view, and always have, that
if you cannot say what you are going
to say in 20 minutes you ought to
go away and write a book about it.

Lord Brabazon

———◆———

Poetry: the best words
in the best order.

Samuel Taylor Coleridge

———◆———

A great many people employed
reading and writing would be
better employed keeping rabbits.

Edith Sitwell

The sheer complexity of writing
a play always had dazzled me.
In an effort to understand
it, I became a critic.

Kenneth Tynan

It is all very well to be able
to write books, but can
you waggle your ears?

J. M. Barrie

One hates an author
that's all author.

Lord Byron

While an author is yet living we estimate his powers by his worst performance, and when he is dead we rate them by his best.

Samuel Johnson

Everything is useful to a writer, you see – every scrap, even the longest and most boring of luncheon parties.

Graham Greene

There is a great discovery still to be made in literature, that of paying literary men by the quantity they do not write.

Thomas Carlyle

Let every bookworm, when in
any fragrant, scarce, old tome
he discovers a sentence, a story,
an illustration, that does his
heart good, hasten to give it.

Samuel Taylor Coleridge

I can't write a book commensurate
with Shakespeare, but I
can write a book by me.

Walter Raleigh

Unprovided with original learning,
unformed in the habits of thinking,
unskilled in the arts of composition,
I resolved to write a book.

Edward Gibbon

We read to know that we are not alone.

C. S. Lewis

BOYS AND GIRLS

They say men can
never experience the
pain of childbirth.
They can if you hit
them in the goolies
for 14 hours.

Jo Brand

Wives are young men's mistresses;
companions for middle age;
and old men's nurses.

Francis Bacon

—•—

Sure men were born to lie,
and women to believe them!

John Gay

—•—

A wise woman puts a grain of
sugar into everything she says to
a man, and takes a grain of salt
with everything he says to her.

Helen Rowland

Men act and women appear. Men
look at women. Women watch
themselves being looked at.

John Berger

───◆───

Some of my best leading men
have been dogs and horses.

Elizabeth Taylor

───◆───

A woman, especially if she has the
misfortune of knowing anything,
should conceal it as well as she can.

Jane Austen

The man's desire is for the woman;
but the woman's desire is rarely
other than for the desire of the man.

Samuel Taylor Coleridge

———•———

Men are judged as the sum
of their parts while women are
judged as some of their parts.

Julie Burchill

———•———

I would rather trust a woman's
instinct than a man's reason.

Stanley Baldwin

I expect that Woman will be the
last thing civilised by Man.

George Meredith

There are always women who
will take men on their own
terms. If I were a man I wouldn't
bother to change while there
are women like that around.

Ann Oakley

It is difficult for a woman
to define her feelings in a
language which is chiefly made
by men to express theirs.

Thomas Hardy

The cocks may
crow, but it's the hen
that lays the egg.

Margaret Thatcher

Men are gentle, honest and
straightforward. Women
are convoluted, deceptive
and dangerous.

Erin Pizzey

As usual, there is a great
woman behind every idiot.

John Lennon

Clever and attractive women
do not want to vote; they are
willing to let men govern as
long as they govern men.

George Bernard Shaw

A man may keep a woman,
but not his estate.

Samuel Richardson

—•—

Most of us women like men, you
know; it's just that we find them
a constant disappointment.

Clare Short

—•—

I cannot be a man with
wishing, therefore I will die
a woman with grieving.

William Shakespeare

The main difference between men and women is that men are lunatics and women are idiots.

Rebecca West

There is very little difference between men and women in space.

Helen Sharman

The silliest woman can manage a clever man; but it needs a clever woman to manage a fool.

Rudyard Kipling

If women were as fastidious as men, morally or physically, there would be an end of the race.

George Bernard Shaw

We women talk too much, nevertheless we only say half of what we know.

Nancy Witcher Astor

I don't suppose any man has
ever understood any woman
since the beginning of things.

H. G. Wells

A woman who looks like a girl and
thinks like a man is the best sort, the
most enjoyable to be and the most
pleasurable to have and to hold.

Julie Burchill

CHEAP SHOTS

Sometimes I
need what only
you can provide
~ your absence.

Ashleigh Brilliant

She had much in common with
Hitler, only no moustache.

Noël Coward

—•—

He brings to the fierce struggle of
politics the tepid enthusiasm of a lazy
summer afternoon at a cricket match.

Aneurin Bevan

—•—

The right honourable gentleman is
reminiscent of a poker. The only
difference is that a poker gives off
the occasional signs of warmth.

Benjamin Disraeli on Robert Peel

I thought men like that
shot themselves.

King George V

———•———

Nature, not content with denying
him the ability to think, has endowed
him with the ability to write.

A. E. Housman

———•———

So boring you fall asleep
halfway through her name.

Alan Bennett

She was a large woman who seemed
not so much dressed as upholstered.

J. M. Barrie

She plunged into a sea of
platitudes, and with the powerful
breaststroke of a channel swimmer,
made her confident way towards
the white cliffs of the obvious.

W. Somerset Maugham

He had occasional flashes of
silence that made his conversation
perfectly delightful.

Sydney Smith

Thou hast no more
brain than I have
in mine elbows.

William Shakespeare

You've got the subtlety of a bullfrog.

H. G. Wells

Why don't you get a haircut?
You look like a chrysanthemum.

P. G. Wodehouse

He couldn't see a belt
without hitting below it.

Margot Asquith on David Lloyd George

Why don't you write books
people can read?

Nora Joyce to her husband James Joyce

Only dull people are
brilliant at breakfast.

Oscar Wilde

Is he just doing a bad Elvis pout,
or was he born that way?

Freddie Mercury on Billy Idol

He would kill his own mother just so
that he could use her skin to make
a drum to beat his own praises.

Margot Asquith on Winston Churchill

He got that scar as a child, when he
fell off his pony on to a silver spoon.

Julie Burchill on Guy Ritchie

His impact on history would be
no more than the whiff of scent
on a lady's handkerchief.

David Lloyd George on Arthur Balfour

The tautness of his face
sours ripe grapes.

William Shakespeare

If Kitchener was not a great man,
he was at least, a great poster.

Margot Asquith

I see her as one great stampede of lips directed at the nearest derrière.

Noël Coward

If I say that he is extremely stupid, I don't mean that in a derogatory sense. I simply mean that he's not very intelligent.

Alan Bennett

DEATH COMES TO US ALL

The idea is to die young as late as possible.

Ashley Montagu

Nothing in his life became
him like the leaving it.

William Shakespeare

Every man dies, but not
every man truly lives.

William Wallace

There's nothing glorious in
dying. Anyone can do it.

Johnny Rotten

Nothing except possibly love
and death are of importance, and
even the importance of death is
somewhat ephemeral, as no one has
yet faxed back a reliable report.

Gerald Durrell

Either that wallpaper goes, or I do.

Oscar Wilde's last words

There is nothing which at once
affects a man so much and
so little as his own death.

Samuel Butler

***

I told you I was ill.

Spike Milligan's epitaph

***

In Liverpool, the difference
between a funeral and a
wedding is one less drunk.

Paul O'Grady

While I thought that
I was learning how
to live, I have been
learning how to die.

Joseph Conrad

Memorial services are the cocktail
parties of the geriatric set.

Harold Macmillan

If you don't go to other people's
funerals, they won't go to yours.

Bob Monkhouse

He'd make a lovely corpse.

Charles Dickens

Life levels all men. Death
reveals the eminent.

George Bernard Shaw

———

I want to die like my father,
peacefully in his sleep, not screaming
and terrified, like his passengers.

Bob Monkhouse

———

Man is a noble animal, splendid in
ashes, and pompous in the grave.

Thomas Browne

At my age I do what Mark Twain
did. I get my daily paper, look
at the obituaries page and if I'm
not in there I carry on as usual.

Patrick Moore

I once got sacked for laughing... mind
you, I was driving a hearse at the time.

Bernard Manning

He is one of those people
who would be enormously
improved by death.

Saki

EDUCATION, EDUCATION, EDUCATION

Education costs money, but then so does ignorance.

Claus Moser

It is no small mischief to a boy,
that many of the best years of
his life should be devoted to the
learning of what can never be of
any real use to any human being.

William Cobbett

———

Spoon-feeding in the long
run teaches us nothing but
the shape of the spoon.

E. M. Forster

———

Education is simply the soul
of a society as it passes from
one generation to another.

G. K. Chesterton

He's very clever, but sometimes
his brains go to his head.

Margot Asquith

———•———

Education is what remains
when we have forgotten all
that we have been taught.

George Savile

———•———

Education makes a people easy to
lead, but difficult to drive; easy to
govern but impossible to enslave.

Henry Peter Brougham

What sculpture is to a block of
marble, education is to a human soul.

Joseph Addison

—◆—

The more scholastically educated
a man is generally, the more
he is an emotional boor.

D. H. Lawrence

—◆—

That's the public-school system
all over. They may kick you out,
but they never let you down.

Evelyn Waugh

If one could only teach the
English how to talk, and the
Irish how to listen, society here
would be quite civilised.

Oscar Wilde

The vanity of teaching
often tempteth a man to
forget he is a blockhead.

George Savile

The great mass of humanity should
never learn to read or write.

D. H. Lawrence

The sum and substance of female
education in America, as in England,
is training women to consider
marriage as the sole object in life, and
to pretend that they do not think so.

Harriet Martineau

Our minds want clothes as
much as our bodies.

Samuel Butler

FASHION OF THE DAY

Never in the history
of fashion has so little
material been raised
so high to reveal so
much that needs to
be covered so badly.

Cecil Beaton

Any man may be in good spirits and
good temper when he's well dressed.
There ain't much credit in that.

Charles Dickens

What a deformed thief
this fashion is.

William Shakespeare

When a popular phenomenon
reaches the cover of *Time*, it
is already out of fashion.

Richard Holloway

Fashion is what you adopt when you don't know who you are.

Quentin Crisp

No man is esteemed for gay garments but by fools and women.

Walter Raleigh

As to matters of dress, I would recommend one never to be first in the fashion nor the last out of it.

John Wesley

I never cared for fashion much,
amusing little seams and witty little
pleats: it was the girls I liked.

David Bailey

Ladies of fashion starve their
happiness to feed their vanity, and
their love to feed their pride.

Charles Caleb Colton

One had as good be out of the
world, as out of the fashion.

Colley Cibber

Happy the society whose deepest
divisions are ones of style.

Peter McKay

I'm not that interested in fashion...
When someone says that lime green
is the new black for this season, you
just want to tell them to get a life.

Bruce Oldfield

Oh, never mind the fashion. When
one has a style of one's own, it
is always twenty times better.

Margaret Oliphant

Looking good and dressing
well is a necessity. Having
a purpose in life is not.

Oscar Wilde

If a woman rebels against high-
heeled shoes, she should take
care to do it in a very smart hat.

George Bernard Shaw

She wore far too much rouge
last night and not quite enough
clothes. That is always a sign
of despair in a woman.

Oscar Wilde

—•—

I'm not here to make people
look like a sack of potatoes.

Alexander McQueen

—•—

I like to make people look as
good as they'd like to look, and
with luck, a shade better.

Norman Parkinson

FOR BETTER AND FOR WORSE

Marriage is a very good thing, but I think it's a mistake to make a habit out of it.

W. Somerset Maugham

A husband is what is left of the lover
after the nerve has been extracted.

Helen Rowland

It is a woman's business to get
married as soon as possible,
and a man's to keep unmarried
as long as possible.

George Bernard Shaw

One was never married, and
that's his hell; another is,
and that's his plague.

Robert Burton

You only require two things in
life: your sanity and your wife.

Tony Blair

What is marriage but prostitution
to one man instead of many?

Angela Carter

Ideally, couples need three
lives; one for him, one for her,
and one for them together.

Jacqueline Bisset

An archeologist is the best husband
any woman can have; the older she
gets, the more interested he is in her.

Agatha Christie

———•———

Love the quest; marriage the
conquest; divorce the inquest.

Helen Rowland

———•———

Good marriages are made in
heaven. Or some such place.

Robert Bolt

The most happy marriage I can
imagine to myself would be the union
of a deaf man to a blind woman.

Samuel Taylor Coleridge

The critical period in matrimony
is breakfast-time.

A. P. Herbert

Marriage is popular because it
combines the maximum of temptation
with the maximum of opportunity.

George Bernard Shaw

For marriage to be a success, every
woman and every man should have
her and his own bathroom. The end.

Catherine Zeta-Jones

Marriage may often be a stormy
lake, but celibacy is almost
always a muddy horse pond.

Thomas Love Peacock

Ireland is a great country
to die or be married in.

Elizabeth Bowen

Bachelors have consciences,
married men have wives.

Samuel Johnson

Marriage is distinctly and
repeatedly excluded from heaven.
Is this because it is thought likely
to mar the general felicity?

Samuel Butler

A bride at her second marriage
does not wear a veil. She wants
to see what she is getting.

Helen Rowland

Happiness in marriage is
entirely a matter of chance.

Jane Austen

—◆·◆—

I never married because there was
no need. I have three pets at home
which answer the same purpose
as a husband. I have a dog which
growls every morning, a parrot
which swears all afternoon, and a
cat that comes home late at night.

Marie Corelli

—◆·◆—

A husband is very much
like a house or a horse.

Anthony Trollope

FRIEND OR FOE?

Thy friendship oft
has made my heart to
ache; do be my enemy,
for friendship's sake.

William Blake

Most people enjoy the inferiority
of their best friends.

Philip Dormer Stanhope

Treat your friends as you
do your pictures, and place
them in their best light.

Jennie Jerome Churchill

Friendship is certainly the
finest balm for the pangs
of disappointed love.

Jane Austen

Where minds differ and
opinions swerve there is scant
a friend in that company.

Queen Elizabeth I

—◆—

A brother may not be a friend, but
a friend will always be a brother.

Samuel Richardson

—◆—

An acquaintance that begins
with a compliment is sure to
develop into a real friendship.

Oscar Wilde

Some people go to priests;
others to poetry; I to my friends.

Virginia Woolf

———————

True friendship is like sound
health; the value of it is seldom
known until it be lost.

Charles Caleb Colton

———————

If I cannot understand my
friend's silence, I will never get
to understand his words.

John Enoch Powell

Hatreds are the cinders of affection.

Walter Raleigh

He's my friend that speaks
well of me behind my back.

Thomas Fuller

Friendship is like money,
easier made than kept.

Samuel Butler

If a man does not make new acquaintance as he advances through life, he will soon find himself left alone. A man, sir, should keep his friendship in constant repair.

Samuel Johnson

Friendship is love without wings.

Lord Byron

If I had to choose between betraying
my country and betraying my
friend, I hope I should have the
guts to betray my country.

E. M. Forster

You find out who your real friends
are when you're involved in a scandal.

Elizabeth Taylor

FULL OF LIFE

Life is like a tin of
sardines – we're all of
us looking for the key.

Alan Bennett

The life of every man is a diary
in which he means to write one
story, and writes another.

J. M. Barrie

❦

Born to lose, live to win.

Lemmy Kilmister

❦

Life is so constructed that an
event does not, cannot, will
not, match the expectation.

Charlotte Brontë

127

Life was a funny thing
that happened to me on
the way to the grave.

Quentin Crisp

The trick in life is learning
how to deal with it.

Helen Mirren

Life is wasted on the living.

Douglas Adams

Life is one
long process of
getting tired.

Samuel Butler

The trouble with the world is
that the stupid are cocksure and
the intelligent full of doubt.

Bertrand Russell

———•———

Life is like playing a violin
solo in public and learning the
instrument as one goes on.

Samuel Butler

———•———

Life is a long lesson in humility.

J. M. Barrie

When we are born, we
cry that we are come
To this great stage of fools.

William Shakespeare

Life is what happens to you while
you're busy making other plans.

John Lennon

We have employment assigned to us
for every circumstance in life. When
we are alone, we have our thoughts
to watch; in the family, our tempers;
and in company, our tongues.

Hannah More

Man alone is born crying, lives complaining, and dies disappointed.

Samuel Johnson

❧

My school days were the happiest days of my life; which should give you some indication of the misery I've endured over the past 25 years.

Paul Merton

❧

To live is the rarest thing in the world. Most people exist, that is all.

George Orwell

We make a living by what we get,
but we make a life by what we give.

Winston Churchill

Life is a sexually transmitted disease.

Guy Bellamy

GETTING ON A BIT

I wanna live till I die,
no more, no less.

Eddie Izzard

Age appears to be best in four
things – old wood best to burn,
old wine to drink, old friends to
trust, and old authors to read.

Francis Bacon

———

I guess I don't so much mind being
old, as I mind being fat and old.

Peter Gabriel

———

You only have to survive in England
and all is forgiven... if you can eat a
boiled egg at 90 in England they
think you deserve a Nobel Prize.

Alan Bennett

One of the best parts of growing older? You can flirt all you like since you've become harmless.

Liz Smith

———

Growing old is compulsory; growing up is optional.

Bob Monkhouse

———

One should never trust a woman who tells her real age. If she tells that, she'll tell anything.

Oscar Wilde

I'm aiming by the time I'm 50 to
stop being an adolescent.

Wendy Cope

—◆—

When you get to 52 food becomes
more important than sex.

Prue Leith

—◆—

You know you are getting old when
the candles cost more than the cake.

Bob Hope

I do wish I could tell you my age but it's impossible. It keeps changing all the time.

Greer Garson

Those who love deeply never grow old; they may die of old age, but they die young.

Arthur Wing Pinero

Young men are apt to think themselves wise enough, as drunken men are apt to think themselves sober enough.

Philip Dormer Stanhope

Life begins at 40 – but so do fallen
arches, rheumatism, faulty eyesight,
and the tendency to tell a story to
the same person, three or four times.

Helen Rowland

I've just become a pensioner
so I've started saving up for
my own hospital trolley.

Tom Baker

Middle age is when your age starts
to show around your middle.

Bob Hope

Age is a very high price
to pay for maturity.

Tom Stoppard

There are three classes into
which all the women past 70 that
ever I knew were to be divided:
1. That dear old soul; 2. That
old woman; 3. That old witch.

Samuel Taylor Coleridge

HAPPY FAMILIES

I saw six men kicking and punching the mother-in-law. My neighbour said 'Are you going to help?' I said 'No, six should be enough.'

Les Dawson

The place of the father in the modern suburban family is a very small one, particularly if he plays golf.

Bertrand Russell

Whether family life is physically harmful is still in dispute.

Keith Waterhouse

We came into the world like brother and brother; and now let's go hand in hand, not one before another.

William Shakespeare

Two women a week are currently
murdered by the man they live with,
and one child by their father or
stepfather. But hey, the family that
slays together stays together.

Julie Burchill

He that has no fools, knaves,
nor beggars in his family was
begot by a flash of lightning.

Thomas Fuller

If you cannot get rid of the
family skeleton, you may
as well make it dance.

George Bernard Shaw

Important families are like potatoes.
The best parts are underground.

Francis Bacon

The voice of parents is the voice
of gods, for to their children
they are heaven's lieutenants.

William Shakespeare

If you don't believe in ghosts then
you've never been to a family reunion.

Ashleigh Brilliant

The awe and dread with which the
untutored savage contemplates his
mother-in-law are amongst the most
familiar facts of anthropology.

James George Frazer

Family jokes, though rightly
cursed by strangers, are the bond
that keeps most families alive.

Stella Benson

JOHNNY FOREIGNER

Admiration for ourselves and our institutions is too often measured by our contempt and dislike for foreigners.

William Ralph Inge

America is a large friendly dog in
a small room. Every time it wags
its tail, it knocks over a chair.

Arnold Joseph Toynbee

I can't even spell spaghetti
never mind talk Italian. How
could I tell an Italian to get the
ball? He might grab mine.

Brian Clough

An English man does not
travel to see English men.

Laurence Sterne

The Irish are a fair people; they never speak well of one another.

Samuel Johnson

A man travels the world in search of what he needs and returns home to find it.

George Moore

You can always count on Americans to do the right thing – after they've tried everything else.

Winston Churchill

England is a paradise for
women and hell for horses; Italy
is a paradise for horses, hell for
women, as the diverb goes.

Robert Burton

Frogs are slightly better than Huns
or Wops, but abroad is unutterably
bloody and foreigners are fiends.

Nancy Mitford

In Mexico an air conditioner is called
a politician because it makes a lot
of noise but doesn't work very well.

Len Deighton

India's a muddle.

E. M. Forster

—•—

They pour themselves one
over the other like so much
melted butter over parsnips.

D. H. Lawrence on Italians

—•—

I love Americans, but not when they
try to talk French. What a blessing it
is that they never try to talk English.

Saki

San Francisco is a mad city
– inhabited for the most part by
perfectly insane people whose
women are of remarkable beauty.

Rudyard Kipling

Apart from cheese and tulips,
the main product of the country is
advocaat, a drink made from lawyers.

Alan Coren on the Netherlands

People travel for
the same reason
they collect works
of art: because the
best people do it.

Aldous Huxley

LET'S GET POLITICAL

A lot has been
said about
politicians; some of
it complimentary, but
most of it accurate.

Eric Idle

The wisdom of hindsight, so
useful to historians and indeed
to authors of memoirs, is sadly
denied to practising politicians.

Margaret Thatcher

Politics are very much like
war. We may even have to
use poison gas at times.

Winston Churchill

A parliament is nothing less
than a big meeting of more
or less idle people.

Walter Bagehot

The Labour Party's election
manifesto is the longest
suicide note in history.

Greg Knight

I have no interest in sailing around
the world. Not that there is any
lack of requests for me to do so.

Edward Heath

If the word 'No' was removed
from the English language, Ian
Paisley would be speechless.

John Hume

If there is one eternal truth
of politics, it is that there
are always a dozen good
reasons for doing nothing.

John le Carré

There is no gambling like politics.

Benjamin Disraeli

He knows nothing and thinks he
knows everything. That clearly
points to a career in politics.

George Bernard Shaw

King Louis Philippe once said to me
that he attributed the great success
of the British nation in political life
to their talking politics after dinner.

Benjamin Disraeli

Our great democracies still tend to
think that a stupid man is more likely
to be honest than a clever man, and
our politicians take advantage of this
prejudice by pretending to be even
more stupid than nature made them.

Bertrand Russell

No man is regular in his
attendance at the House of
Commons until he is married.

Benjamin Disraeli

Instead of giving a politician
the keys to the city, it might be
better to change the locks.

Doug Larson

The best time to listen to a politician
is when he's on a stump on a street
corner in the rain late at night when
he's exhausted. Then he doesn't lie.

Theodore H. White

I remain just one thing, and one thing only, and that is a clown. It places me on a far higher plane than any politician.

Charlie Chaplin

The proper memory for a politician is one that knows what to remember and what to forget.

John Morley

The difference between a
misfortune and a calamity is this: if
Gladstone fell into the Thames,
it would be a misfortune. But if
someone dragged him out again,
that would be a calamity.

Benjamin Disraeli

Politics is a blood sport.

Aneurin Bevan

Politics is the art of looking for trouble, finding it whether it exists or not, diagnosing it incorrectly, and applying the wrong remedy.

Ernest Benn

You slam a politician, you make out he's the devil, with horns and hoofs. But his wife loves him, and so did all his mistresses.

Pamela Hansford Johnson

The politician who never made a mistake never made a decision.

John Major

We all know that prime ministers
are wedded to the truth, but
like other wedded couples
they sometimes live apart.

Saki

Anybody who enjoys being in the
House of Commons probably
needs psychiatric care.

Ken Livingstone

You can't be in
politics unless you
can walk in a room
and know in a minute
who's for you and
who's against you.

Samuel Johnson

THE L-WORD

Love is like the measles – all the worse when it comes late in life.

Douglas Jerrod

To fear love is to fear life,
and those who fear life are
already three parts dead.

Bertrand Russell

When my love swears that
she is made of truth,
I do believe her though
I know she lies.

William Shakespeare

Absence – that common cure of love.

Lord Byron

How absurd and delicious to be in love with somebody younger than yourself. Everybody should try it.

Barbara Pym

Love is only a dirty trick played on us to achieve continuation of the species.

W. Somerset Maugham

THE L-WORD

Love is an act of endless
forgiveness; a tender look
which becomes a habit.

Peter Ustinov

—•—

A mistress never is nor can
be a friend. While you agree,
you are lovers; and when it is
over, anything but friends.

Lord Byron

—•—

If you live to be a hundred, I want to
live to be a hundred minus one day
so I never have to live without you.

A. A. Milne

No woman ever hates a man
for being in love with her, but
many a woman hates a man
for being a friend to her.

Alexander Pope

Love is a wonderful, terrible thing.

William Shakespeare

Love comes unseen;
we only see it go.

Austin Dobson

THE L-WORD

Whatever our souls are made
of, his and mine are the same.

Emily Brontë

Who ever loved that loved
not at first sight?

Christopher Marlowe

A loving heart is the beginning
of all knowledge.

Thomas Carlyle

The simple lack of her is more
to me than others' presence.

Edward Thomas

Love is my religion – I could die for it.

John Keats

MANNERS MAKETH MAN

Nothing more rapidly
inclines a person to go
into a monastery than
reading a book on
etiquette. There are
so many trivial ways in
which it is possible to
commit some social sin.

Quentin Crisp

Whatever it is that makes a person charming, it needs to remain a mystery... once the charmer is aware of a mannerism or characteristic that others find charming, it ceases to be a mannerism and becomes an affectation. And good Lord, there is nothing less charming than affectations!

Rex Harrison

The English are polite by telling lies. The Americans are polite by telling the truth.

Malcolm Bradbury

A man's own good breeding
is his best security against
other people's ill-manners.

Philip Dormer Stanhope

I do not want people to be very
agreeable, as it saves me the
trouble of liking them a great deal.

Jane Austen

It is more comfortable for me, in the
long run, to be rude than polite.

Wyndham Lewis

Manners are especially the
need of the plain. The pretty
can get away with anything.

Evelyn Waugh

In proceeding to the dining
room, the gentleman gives one
arm to the lady he escorts – it
is unusual to offer both.

Lewis Carroll

Talk to every woman as if you loved
her, and to every man as if he bored
you, and at the end of your first
season you will have the reputation of
possessing the most perfect social tact.

Oscar Wilde

And though it is much to
be a nobleman, it is more
to be a gentleman.

Anthony Trollope

Whoever one is, and wherever
one is, one is always in the
wrong if one is rude.

Maurice Baring

Civility costs nothing and
buys everything.

Lady Mary Wortley Montagu

At a dinner party one should
eat wisely but not too well, and
talk well but not too wisely.

W. Somerset Maugham

We don't bother much about
dress and manners in England,
because as a nation we don't dress
well and we've got no manners.

George Bernard Shaw

MEDIA MEDDLING

The media. It sounds
like a convention
of spiritualists.

Tom Stoppard

What the mass media offers is not popular art, but entertainment which is intended to be consumed like food, forgotten and replaced by a new dish.

W. H. Auden

Television has brought back murder into the home – where it belongs.

Alfred Hitchcock

Media is a word that
has come to mean
bad journalism.

Graham Greene

I review novels to make money, because it is easier for a sluggard to write an article a fortnight than a book a year, because the writer is soothed by the opiate of action, the crank by posing as a good journalist, and having an air hole.

Cyril Connolly

A book may be compared to your neighbour: if it be good, it cannot last too long; if bad, you cannot get rid of it too early.

Rupert Brooke

A petty reason perhaps why
novelists more and more try to
keep a distance from journalists
is that novelists are trying to
write the truth and journalists
are trying to write fiction.

Graham Greene

———•———

[Television] is a medium of
entertainment which permits
millions of people to listen to
the same joke at the same time,
and yet remain lonesome.

T. S. Eliot

Journalists say a thing that
they know isn't true, in the hope
that if they keep on saying it
long enough it will be true.

Arnold Bennett

He who is created by television
can be destroyed by television.

Theodore H. White

If everyone demanded peace
instead of another television
set, then there'd be peace.

John Lennon

Reading someone else's newspaper is like sleeping with someone else's wife. Nothing seems to be precisely in the right place, and when you find what you are looking for, it is not clear then how to respond to it.

Malcolm Bradbury

Seeing a murder on television can help work off one's antagonisms. And if you haven't any antagonisms, the commercials will give you some.

Alfred Hitchcock

The most important service rendered by the press and the magazines is that of educating people to approach printed matter with distrust.

Samuel Butler

To read a newspaper is to refrain from reading something worthwhile.

Aleister Crowley

For fear of the newspapers, politicians are dull, and at last they are too dull even for the newspapers.

G. K. Chesterton

Journalism is literature in a hurry.

Matthew Arnold

NINE TO FIVE

The employer
generally gets
the employees
he deserves.

Walter Raleigh

It is not real work unless you would
rather be doing something else.

J. M. Barrie

The best way to appreciate your job
is to imagine yourself without one.

Oscar Wilde

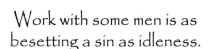

Work with some men is as
besetting a sin as idleness.

Samuel Butler

I like work; it fascinates me. I can sit and look at it for hours. I love to keep it by me; the idea of getting rid of it nearly breaks my heart.

Jerome K. Jerome

You'll never succeed in idealising hard work. Before you can dig mother earth you've got to take off your ideal jacket. The harder a man works, at brute labour, the thinner becomes his idealism, the darker his mind.

D. H. Lawrence

Work is life, you know, and
without it, there's nothing
but fear and insecurity.

John Lennon

The reward of labour is
life. Is that not enough?

William Morris

If you have great talents, industry
will improve them: if you have
but moderate abilities, industry
will supply their deficiency.

Joshua Reynolds

If you want creative workers,
give them enough time to play.

John Cleese

Business opportunities are
like buses – there's always
another one coming.

Richard Branson

It is very vulgar to talk about
one's business. Only people
like stockbrokers do that, and
then merely at dinner parties.

Oscar Wilde

One of the symptoms of an
approaching nervous breakdown
is the belief that one's work
is terribly important.

Bertrand Russell

It is the job that is never started
that takes longest to finish.

J. R. R. Tolkien

PENNIES AND POUNDS

Pennies do not come
from heaven. They
have to be earned
here on earth.

Margaret Thatcher

Broke is a temporary condition,
poor is a state of mind.

Richard Francis Burton

Money is like muck, not good
except it be spread.

Francis Bacon

Money is the source of the
greatest vice, and that nation
which is most rich, is most wicked.

Frances Burney

Money is like a sixth sense
without which you cannot make a
complete use of the other five.

W. Somerset Maugham

Money couldn't buy friends, but
you got a better class of enemy.

Spike Milligan

Having money is rather like being a
blonde. It is more fun but not vital.

Mary Quant

Short accounts make long friends.

Anthony Trollope

The more I see of the
moneyed classes, the more I
understand the guillotine.

George Bernard Shaw

The honest poor can sometimes
forget poverty. The honest
rich can never forget it.

G. K. Chesterton

A poor man is despised
the whole world over.

Jerome K. Jerome

***

Whereas it has long been known
and declared that the poor have
no right to the property of the
rich, I wish it also to be known and
declared that the rich have no right
to the property of the poor.

John Ruskin

***

I was born with a plastic
spoon in my mouth.

Pete Townshend

A beggar that is dumb, you know,
May challenge double pity.

Walter Raleigh

Love lasteth long as the
money endureth.

William Caxton

An agent is a person who is
sore because an actor gets 90
per cent of what they make.

Elton John

A large income is the best recipe
for happiness I ever heard of.

Jane Austen

In many walks of life, a conscience
is a more expensive encumbrance
than a wife or a carriage.

Thomas de Quincey

A thing is worth what it can
do for you, not what you
choose to pay for it.

John Ruskin

SCIENTIFICALLY SPEAKING

There comes a time
when every scientist,
even God, has to write
off an experiment.

P. D. James

Science has its being in a
perpetual mental restlessness.

William Temple

A computer terminal is not
some clunky old television with
a typewriter in front of it. It is an
interface where the mind and body
can connect with the universe
and move bits of it about.

Douglas Adams

Logic is neither a science
or an art, but a dodge.

Benjamin Jowett

It requires a very unusual
mind to undertake the
analysis of the obvious.

Alfred North Whitehead

———•———

New ideas pass through three
periods: 1) It can't be done. 2)
It probably can be done, but
it's not worth doing. 3) I knew
it was a good idea all along!

Arthur C. Clarke

———•———

The complex develops
out of the simple.

Colin Wilson

Science is the great antidote
to the poison of enthusiasm
and superstition.

Adam Smith

——————•——————

Ignorance more frequently begets
confidence than does knowledge: it is
those who know little, and not those
who know much, who so positively
assert that this or that problem
will never be solved by science.

Charles Darwin

Science, after all, is only an
expression for our ignorance
of our own ignorance.

Samuel Butler

Science in the modern world
has many uses; its chief use,
however, is to provide long words
to cover the errors of the rich.

G. K. Chesterton

It is a safe rule to apply that, when
a mathematical or philosophical
author writes with a misty
profundity, he is talking nonsense.

Alfred North Whitehead

In everything that relates to
science, I am a whole encyclopaedia
behind the rest of the world.

Charles Lamb

—•—

I don't believe in astrology; I'm a
Sagittarius and we're sceptical.

Arthur C. Clarke

—•—

In science there are many matters
about which people are agreed;
in philosophy there are none.

Bertrand Russell

The great tragedy of science:
the slaying of a beautiful
hypothesis by an ugly fact.

Thomas Henry Huxley

Before a war military science
seems like a real science, like
astronomy; but after a war it
seems more like astrology.

Rebecca West

TAKE MY ADVICE

Advice is seldom
welcome, and those
who need it the most,
like it the least.

Lord Chesterfield

Judge not others
unless you're
prepared to
be judged!

Johnny Rotten

He that gives good advice,
builds with one hand; he that
gives good counsel and example,
builds with both; but he that
gives good admonition and bad
example, builds with one hand
and pulls down with the other.

Francis Bacon

Have the courage to be ignorant
of a great number of things, in
order to avoid the calamity of
being ignorant of everything.

Sydney Smith

No one can take less pains than to hold his tongue. Hear much, and speak little; for the tongue is the instrument of the greatest good and greatest evil that is done in the world.

Walter Raleigh

The only way to be sure of catching a train is to miss the one before it.

G. K. Chesterton

Good but rarely came from good advice.

Lord Byron

A woman seldom asks advice before she has bought her wedding clothes.

Joseph Addison

———

We ask advice, but we mean approbation.

Charles Caleb Colton

———

Moderation is a fatal thing – nothing succeeds like excess.

Oscar Wilde

When a man wants your advice,
he generally wants your praise.

Lord Chesterfield

Love all, trust a few,
do wrong to none.

William Shakespeare

Don't give a woman advice; one
should never give a woman anything
she can't wear in the evening.

Oscar Wilde

The worst men often
give the best advice.

Francis Bacon

———•———

I owe my success to having
listened respectfully to the very
best advice, and then going away
and doing the exact opposite.

G. K. Chesterton

Never try to reason the prejudice out of a man. It was not reasoned into him, and cannot be reasoned out.

Sydney Smith

Remember, you can always stoop and pick up nothing.

Charlie Chaplin

After 40 a woman has
to choose between
losing her figure or
her face. My advice
is to keep your face,
and stay sitting down.

Barbara Cartland

THE TROUBLE WITH SIN

All sins tend to
be addictive, and
the terminal point
of addiction is
damnation.

W. H. Auden

The greatest art of a politician
is to render vice serviceable
to the cause of virtue.

Henry Bolingbroke

A sense of humour keen enough
to show a man his own absurdities
will keep him from the commission
of all sins, or nearly all, save
those worth committing.

Samuel Butler

A community is infinitely more
brutalised by the habitual
employment of punishment
than it is by the occasional
occurrence of crime.

Oscar Wilde

For God's sake, if you
sin, take pleasure in it,
And do it for the pleasure.

Gerald Gould

—◆—

The problem with people who have
no vices is that generally you can
be pretty sure they're going to have
some pretty annoying virtues.

Elizabeth Taylor

—◆—

I'm an old sinner. Nothing shocks me.

Charlie Chaplin

How like herrings and onions
our vices are in the morning after
we have committed them.

Samuel Taylor Coleridge

———◆———

He that falls into sin is a man;
that grieves at it, is a saint; that
boasteth of it, is a devil.

Thomas Fuller

———◆———

Forbear to judge, for
we are sinners all.

William Shakespeare

Vice, in its true light, is so deformed, that it shocks us at first sight; and would hardly ever seduce us, if it did not at first wear the mask of some virtue.

Lord Chesterfield

Every day confirms my opinion on the superiority of a vicious life – and if virtue is not its own reward I don't know any other stipend annexed to it.

Lord Byron

One leak will sink a ship: and one sin will destroy a sinner.

John Bunyan

He who is only just, is cruel. Who on earth could live were all judged justly?

Lord Byron

—◆—

Flippancy, the most hopeless form of intellectual vice.

George Gissing

—◆—

Sin is geographical.

Bertrand Russell

The function of vice is to keep
virtue within reasonable bounds.

Samuel Butler

If there were no bad people, there
would be no good lawyers.

Charles Dickens

Let them show me a cottage where
there are not the same vices of
which they accuse the courts.

Lord Chesterfield

As one reads history... one is
absolutely sickened, not by
the crimes that the wicked have
committed, but by the punishments
that the good have inflicted.

Oscar Wilde

VIRTUOUS WAYS

Virtue is a beautiful
thing in woman when
they don't go about
with it like a child with
a drum making all
sorts of noise with it.

Douglas Jerrold

Assume a virtue if you have not it.

William Shakespeare

He who stops being better,
stops being good.

Oliver Cromwell

The deadliest foe to virtue would
be complete self-knowledge.

F. H. Bradley

I always admired virtue – but
I could never imitate it.

King Charles II

I you pretend to be good, the
world takes you very seriously.
If you pretend to be bad, it
doesn't. Such is the astounding
stupidity of optimism.

Oscar Wilde

All art is a struggle to be, in a
particular sort of way, virtuous.

Iris Murdoch

Good and bad men are each
less so than they seem.

Samuel Taylor Coleridge

Virtue is more to be feared than vice,
because its excesses are not subject
to the regulation of conscience.

Adam Smith

Nobody shoots at Santa Claus.

Samuel Butler

Virtue is too often merely local.

Samuel Johnson

Oh, blameless people are
always the most exasperating!

George Eliot

No one would remember the Good Samaritan if he'd only had good intentions – he had money too.

Margaret Thatcher

Plenty of people wish to
become devout, but no one
wishes to be humble.

Joseph Addison

❧

Virtue is its own punishment.

Aneurin Bevan

❧

Goodness is beauty
in its best estate.

Christopher Marlowe

What, after all, is a halo? It's only
one more thing to keep clean.

Christopher Fry

———•———

Vices and virtues are of a strange
nature, for the more we have
the fewer we think we have.

Alexander Pope

———•———

In England the only homage which
they pay to virtue – is hypocrisy.

Lord Byron

On the whole, human beings
want to be good, but not too
good, and not quite all the time.

George Orwell

Moderation has been called a virtue
to limit the ambition of great men,
and to console undistinguished
people for their want of fortune
and their lack of merit.

Benjamin Disraeli

If goodness were only a
theory, it were a pity it should
be lost to the world.

William Hazlitt

Blessed is the man who, having nothing to say, abstains from giving us wordy evidence of the fact.

George Eliot

If he does really think that there is no distinction between virtue and vice, why, Sir, when he leaves our houses let us count our spoons.

Samuel Johnson

Men should not try to overstrain their goodness more than any other faculty, bodily or mental.

Samuel Butler

WHAT'S YOUR POISON?

A man's true
character comes out
when he's drunk.

Charlie Chaplin

And wine can of their
wits the wise beguile,
Make the sage frolic, and
the serious smile.

Alexander Pope

I never remember holding a full drink.
My first look shows the
level half-way down.

Philip Larkin

A good local pub
has much in common
with a church, except
that a pub is warmer,
and there's more
conversation.

William Blake

When I played drunks I had to remain sober because I didn't know how to play them when I was drunk.

Richard Burton

———•———

Real ale fans are just like trainspotters, only drunk.

Christopher Howse

———•———

It is immoral to get drunk because the headache comes after the drinking, but if the headache came first and the drunkenness afterwards, it would be moral to get drunk.

Samuel Butler

Alcohol is a very necessary article.
It enables Parliament to do things at
eleven at night that no sane person
would do at eleven in the morning.

George Bernard Shaw

Bring in the bottled lightning, a
clean tumbler, and a corkscrew.

Charles Dickens

The first draught serveth for health,
the second for pleasure, the third
for shame, the fourth for madness.

Walter Raleigh

Fill it up. I take as large draughts
of liquor as I did of love. I
hate a flincher in either.

John Gay

———— ·•· ————

This is one of the disadvantages
of wine; it makes a man mistake
words for thoughts.

Samuel Johnson

———— ·•· ————

I'm not a heavy drinker; I
can sometimes go for hours
without touching a drop.

Noël Coward

It is widely held that too much
wine will dull a man's desire.
Indeed it will – in a dull man.

John Osborne

I do not live in the world of sobriety.

Oliver Reed

Drink is the feast of reason
and the flow of soul.

Alexander Pope

In my opinion, most of the great
men of the past were only there for
the beer – the wealth, prestige and
grandeur that went with the power.

A. J. P. Taylor

There are some sluggish men
who are improved by drinking;
as there are fruits that are not
good until they are rotten.

Samuel Johnson

I can resist everything
except temptation.

Oscar Wilde

THE YOUTH OF TODAY

I am not young enough
to know everything.

J. M. Barrie

The young always have the same
problem – how to rebel and conform
at the same time. They have now
solved this by defying their parents
and copying one another.

Quentin Crisp

Young blood must have
its course, lad,
And every dog his day.

Charles Kingsley

Every thing is pretty that is young.

Samuel Richardson

Youth is the time of getting, middle age of improving, and old age of spending.

Anne Bradstreet

There is something so amiable in the prejudices of a young mind, that one is sorry to see them give way to the reception of more general opinions.

Jane Austen

A man loves the meat in his youth that he cannot endure in his age.

William Shakespeare

Youth [is] a period of
missed opportunities.

Cyril Connolly

Young men and young women meet
each other with much less difficulty
than was formerly the case, and
every housemaid expects at least
once a week as much excitement as
would have lasted a Jane Austen
heroine throughout a whole novel.

Bertrand Russell

What Youth deemed crystal,
Age finds out was dew.

Robert Browning

———••———

No young man ever
thinks he shall die.

William Hazlitt

———••———

Young people have a marvellous
faculty of either dying or adapting
themselves to circumstances.

Samuel Butler

Human nature is so well disposed towards those who are in interesting situations, that a young person, who either marries or dies, is sure of being kindly spoken of.

Jane Austen

We are none of us infallible – not even the youngest of us.

William Thompson

The excesses of our
youth are checks
written against our
age and they are
payable with interest
30 years later.

Charles Caleb Colton

YOU'VE GOTTA HAVE FAITH

My idea of heaven
is eating pâté de
foie gras to the
sound of trumpets.

Sydney Smith

Religion is the fashionable
substitute for belief.

Oscar Wilde

———•———

So far as I can remember, there
is not one word in the Gospels
in praise of intelligence.

Bertrand Russell

———•———

A saint is one who makes
goodness attractive.

Laurence Houseman

The belief in a supernatural source
of evil is not necessary; men are
quite capable of every wickedness.

Joseph Conrad

The religion of one seems
madness unto another.

Thomas Browne

No mention of God. They
keep Him up their sleeves for
as long as they can, vicars do.
They know it puts people off.

Alan Bennett

Fear of things invisible is the
natural seed of that which everyone
in himself calleth religion.

Thomas Hobbes

And God said, 'Let there be light'
and there was light, but the electricity
board said He would have to wait
until Thursday to be connected.

Spike Milligan

The more I study religions the
more I am convinced that man never
worshipped anything but himself.

Richard Burton

He wears his faith but as
the fashion of his hat.

William Shakespeare

If there were no God, there
would be no atheists.

G. K. Chesterton

And you poor creatures – who
conjured you out of the clay? Is
God in show business, too?

John Boorman

Why should we take advice on sex from the Pope? If he knows anything about it, he shouldn't!

George Bernard Shaw

The worst of madmen
is a saint run mad.

Alexander Pope

Aim at heaven and you will get earth thrown in. Aim at earth and you get neither.

C. S. Lewis

I am ready to meet with my
Maker. Whether my Maker
is prepared for the ordeal of
meeting me is another matter.

Winston Churchill

A good sermon should be like a
woman's skirt: short enough to
arouse interest but long enough
to cover the essentials.

Ronald Knox

I simply haven't the nerve to imagine
a being, a force, a cause which keeps
the planets revolving in their orbits
and then suddenly stops in order to
give me a bicycle with three speeds.

Quentin Crisp

When did I realise I was God?
Well, I was praying and I suddenly
realised I was talking to myself.

Peter O'Toole